PERSPECTIVES ON A GRAFTED TREE

PERSPECTIVES ON A GRAFTED TREE

Thoughts for those touched by adoption

compiled by
PATRICIA IRWIN JOHNSTON

illustrated by
Diana L. Stanley

PERSPECTIVES PRESS

Published by Perspectives Press
    P. O. Box 90318
    Indianapolis, Indiana 46290-0318
Manufactured in the United States of America

ISBN 0-9609504-0-0

The editor gratefully acknowledges the following:

Michael Anderson "Welcome Home" © 1976 Hallmark Cards, Inc. from Childhood Memories. Used by permission.

Leslie Brooke "Mary Cassatt's Mothers and Children" reprinted by permission of the Scholastic Writing Awards Program. Copyright © 1982 by Scholastic Inc.

Mary Anne Cohen ("Agency Poem," "Confession," "Sea Poem") is one of a large number of birthmothers for whom adoption has been a bitter, painful, and negative experience, not really a free choice, or a good choice. She now spends much of her time as an activist in the adoption reform movement, trying to fight what she believes to be a cruel, exploitive, and corrupt system.

Kahlil Gibran "On Children" reprinted from The Prophet by permission of Alfred A. Knopf, Inc. Copyright 1923, renewed 1951 by C.T.A. Administrators of the Kahlil Gibran Estate and Mary G. Gibran.

Fleur Conkling Heyliger "Not Flesh of My Flesh" reprinted from The Saturday Evening Post, © 1952 The Curtis Publishing Company.

Jane Merchant "The Family Tree" from Halfway Up the Sky, copyright renewal © 1981 by Elizabeth Merchant. Used by Permission of the publisher, Abingdon Press.

Carol Lynn Pearson "Little Spirit to Childless Couple" and "To An Adopted" from The Search. Copyright © 1970 by Carol Lynn Pearson. Reprinted by permission of Doubleday and Company, Inc.

Rabindranath Tagore "The Beginning" and "Benediction" reprinted with permission of Macmillan Publishing Co., Inc. from Collected Poems and Plays of Rabindranath Tagore. Copyright 1913 by Macmillan, renewed 1941 by Rabindranath Tagore.

The authors of "Some May Be Born . . .", "Legacy of an Adopted Child," and "The Heart of a Child," were diligently sought both in library indices and through various adoption-related groups' members' sources. The authors remain unknown to the editor, who welcomes their identification for acknowledgement in future printings of Perspectives on a Grafted Tree.

To
Perry and Helen, Phil and Jean,
strong roots,

and to

Joel and Erica,
tender shoots,
of our grafted tree

ACKNOWLEDGMENTS

A book begins like any plant, as a seed in the soil of its author's mind. PERSPECTIVES ON A GRAFTED TREE was a seed which lay dormant in the minds of many of those who submitted pieces for it. The fact that it germinated, rooted and grew here is due to the nurturing that came from those who encouraged me to follow my heart and begin - Dave Johnston, Carol Hallenbeck, Sue Schneider.

The actual fertilization of the tree, however, was done by the groups who willingly and without payment printed a notice to their members and readers in their newsletters and magazines that I was seeking poetry to include in such a volume. To the staffs of Association for the Rights of Children of Indiana (ARC), the Child Welfare League of America, Concerned United Birthparents, Eastern Nebraska RESOLVE, Families Adopting Children from Everywhere (FACE), Families for Children, Feminists Writers Guild, Happiness Holding Tank, Indiana RESOLVE, Inc., North American Council on Adoptable Children, News of OURS, Poets and Writers' CODA, Pudding, and RESOLVE, Inc., I am most grateful. Other groups, too, seem, unbeknownst to me and therefore unacknowledged, to have picked up the announcement as they shared each other's newsletters in the vast adoption network. This book would have been impossible without those generous bits of publicity.

In the warmth of the summer sun, the seedling flourished and finally bloomed. All the while, my ever patient family watched and nodded their encouragement as I typed away trying to meet deadlines so that I could gamble with our precious savings in order to self publish this book after it had been rejected or overlooked by large publishing houses, who considered either its genre - poetry - or its audience - those touched by adoption - either too limited or too risky for them.

And so you hold in your hands my harvest - a sapling straight and tall and proud. May it shade, shelter and support you as you gain your own perspective on the grafted tree that is adoption.

PIJ
Fort Wayne, Indiana
September, 1982

TABLE OF CONTENTS

And a woman who held a babe against her bosom said, speak to us of children.

And he said:

Your children are not your children.
They are the sons and daughters of Life's longing for itself.
They come through you but not from you.
And though they are with you, yet they belong not to you.

You may give them your love but not your thoughts.
For they have their own thoughts.
You may house their bodies, but not their souls,
For their souls dwell in the house of tomorrow, which you cannot
    visit, not even in your dreams.
You may strive to be like them, but seek not to make them like you.
For life goes not backward nor tarries with yesterday.

You are the bows from which your children as living arrows are
    sent forth.
The archer sees the mark upon the path of the infinite, and He
    bends you with His might that His arrows might go swift and far.
Let your bending in the archer's hand be for gladness,
For even as He loves the arrow that flies, so He loves also the bow
    that is stable.

Kahlil Gibran, 1883-1931
Syria
from The Prophet

perspective, n.- the relationship of the parts of a subject to each other and to a whole.

graft, v.- to unite with a growing plant by insertion or placing in close contact.

adoption, n.- the process of accepting the responsibility for raising an individual who has two sets of parents.[1]

This book began as a project of the heart. I am by training, interest, and experience an English instructor and librarian. The written word has always fascinated me, and poetry is a special interest of mine because, when it is well done, it crystallizes experience, capturing in beautiful imagery and few words the essence of human feeling. Some time ago, while our oldest child was yet a baby, I realized that while I had seen many lovely poems addressing adoption themes, those poems were not collected in any accessible place, and that several of them, though widely recognized in adoption circles, were quoted differently in each source and were often attributed to unknown authors. How lovely, I thought, to have an anthology of such poems - a collection of beautiful, positive thoughts for sharing with our children, who were adopted, which would reflect the overwhelmingly positive influence that adoption has had on the lives of my husband (who also happens to be an adoptee) and myself.

That original idea has changed somewhat as I have grown. I was born into a family which had not experienced adoption from any perspective for several generations. My view of adoption before I was married was a very stereotypical one, I am certain. It has been many years, and I've changed and grown so much over that time that I cannot tell you exactly what my adoption perception was, but I recall that I made several rather widely held myths a part of my "knowledge" of adoption. The myths formed this commonly known scenario filled with the phraseology of negative adoption language:

Once upon a time a pair of undereducated teenagers "got caught" with a pregnancy after engaging in an illicit sexual relationship that was purely physical and involved no emotion other than puppy love. In order to "do the right thing," this couple (or more likely just the girl and her parents - since the stereotypical teenaged father had probably already gone his irresponsible way), with the help of a kindly and supportive social worker who carefully laid out all of the options for them without offering any personal bias, "put the baby up for adoption" by an older, wiser, more financially stable barren couple, who, though "denied their own children," took this "poor, rejected infant" to their breasts to nurture "as if s/he were their own."

Meanwhile, the teenagers went on to improve their lives, marry others, and have other children. With a form of selective amnesia they forgot entirely their "unwanted mistake," burying their "shameful pasts" in anonymity as they became productive members of society.

This left the adoptive parents and their child to build a happy family life together, where they would forget the fact of adoption and successfully blend "like a real family" into the community. The children, if they "truly loved their parents," would never feel or express any curiosity about their genetic history or the events which took them from their "real parents" and brought them to their adoptive family.

This scenario was from the uninformed viewpoint of one totally untouched by adoption. My perspective on adoption began to change first when I married into a family in which, of the six cousins added to the family tree in my husband's generation, four of them - including my husband and his sister - had been adopted.

The connection began to expand my horizons concerning adoption. First there was the revelation that, while I was married to a man who feels quite sure of his own identity and has not at any point had an interest in learning more about his biological heritage, there are many adoptees for whom such information is terribly important. Most of this last group are not searching for a set of parents different from those who raised them. Some have medical problems for which a more complete genetic history might be valuable. For others the curiosity of what a biologically connected person might look like triggers this need. For some, the barrier of secrecy surrounding adoption itself causes questions about just what could be so "bad" to demand such strong opinion that the doors should be forever left closed.

My husband and I then faced a family building crisis, when it became apparent that we were dealing with our own infertility. Unlike many infertile couples, we had no problem coming to see adoption as an acceptable and very positive alternative to our childlessness, but we were faced with a closing adoption door. What we wanted then was a baby of the same race as we, and there weren't many available for adoption anymore. Statistics on adoptive placement as an alternative to dealing with a problem pregnancy have completely reversed themselves in less than a decade. Where once nine of ten unmarried mothers made adoption plans for their children, now this is the case with fewer than four in one hundred single mothers whose pregnancies were unplanned. Twenty-five couples wait for each baby available for adoption. We were fortunate to adopt a beautiful son, but we didn't consider our family building complete, and as we experienced further frustration in trying to adopt again, my growth continued.

For nearly four years after I co-founded the group, I was president of Indiana RESOLVE, Inc., a unique statewide network of a national organization offering support, referral, counseling, education, and advocacy services to people dealing with a fertility impairment and its several alternatives - one of which is adoption. This nearly full time volunteer position introduced me to many new ideas and vastly altered my still rather narrow view of adoption as I became involved with other groups which also had an adoption interest. Twice I have been chairperson of an event called "Adoption Forum" - a day-long series of eighteen minisessions on adoption-related topics from agency adoption to private placement, from feelings of birthparents to how to begin a search, from placements of older children or sibling groups to legal issues of the open records controversy. "Adoption Forum" has been developed each time by a planning committee composed of representatives of all of those groups and agencies in our community of over 175,000 people which serve those touched by adoption. They have included our child placing agencies, Lutheran Social Services and Catholic Social Services; our Mental Health Center; the birthparent/adoptee search group called Search for Tomorrow; a support, education and referral group for adoptive families, Association for the Rights of Children; and RESOLVE. The working together of these groups has brought to each of them a heightened sensitivity to and understanding of one another's fears, needs, goals.

Also as president of RESOLVE I have been involved in curriculum development for a series of infant care, child development and special issues classes for adoptive parents-to-be which we call "Our Own Child." Coordinated and developed by Carol Hallenbeck, B.S., R.N., Indiana RESOLVE's other co-founder, the "Our Own Child" series is offered throughout the state and is taught in each city by an adoptive parent with a background in nursing, education, counseling, or social work.

Individually I have been a member of a Fort Wayne coalition called the Adolescent Pregnancy Awareness and Concern Task Force. As an adoptive parent of two children placed as infants, my husband I are members of Association for the Rights of Children locally and subscribe to long distance memberships in Families Adopting Children from Everywhere (FACE) and OURS (Organization for a United Response). Thus we know many other families expanded by adoption to include not just healthy infants, but older children; children who are emotionally, physically or mentally handicapped; sibling groups; and children who are racially different than their parents. The vast majority of ARC parents did not adopt for reasons of infertility, and their families include both biological and adopted children.

My orientation to the written word has brought dozens of books into our home which deal with various perspectives on adoption, and we subscribe to several newsletters and magazines dealing with this theme, too. It was from an accumulation of several years' worth of omnivorous reading that I very selectively put together the list of resources and readings for this book.

All of these experiences over seventeen years have vastly altered my original misconceived view of adoption. Now I know, as I hope do you, that adoption is an institution broad in spectrum and widely misunderstood. Every adoption involves a triad of people - a set of birthparents, an adoptee, and adoptive parent(s). Each member of the adoption triangle experiences unique gains and losses as a result of the adoption experience. While there are unmarried, teenaged birthparents, there are also mature single parents and even married couples who make adoption plans for their birth children. Not all of these children are adopted as newborns, since many birthparents try to parent for some time before deciding to make an adoption plan. In some cases children find their way to adoptive homes after parental rights have been terminated involuntarily through the legal system after instances of abuse and neglect. In some instances parental rights are terminated after much pressure by family members and often, too, parental rights are retained by unwilling parents due to the same kind of pressure. Many adoptive parents are infertile and many of those seek only healthy infants, but other adoptive parents have several biological children and actively seek out children who are handicapped in some way or are of a different racial heritage than their own or are part of a sibling group. Some adoptive parents today are single.

In the center of this, and of utmost importance, is the child for whom an adoption plan has been made. As they grow, finding and exploring their own identities as do all adolescents, adoptees almost always feel some degree of curiosity about the origins of their birth. For some, this adolescent coming of age or some subsequent life experience may trigger a need to seek out more complete information and perhaps even contact with a birthparent. The studies of John Triseliotis of the use made of the open adoption records of Scotland found that fewer than 5% of adoptees chose to make use of the records, and of those who did search the records, well over half had been raised in families where the fact of adoption was not shared until they were adolescents.[2] While this study is sometimes interpretted to indicate that most adoptees with whom the fact of adoption has been shared from the beginning won't want to search, it is unfair to make such a general assumption - to develop such an absolute.

Sociologist H. David Kirk in his works Shared Fate and Adoptive Kinship has introduced the concept of role handicap. Everyone, says Kirk, expects to fill certain roles in his life, each of which carries with it a set of societal expectations. When we assume a life role without being able to assume with it all of the role's expectations, we experience what Kirk calls a role handicap. Both adoptive parents and adopted children, writes Kirk, assume handicapped familial roles; and only by acknowledging the differences from societal norms in their family relationship and with that accepting that each of them, while deriving substantial gains, has also experienced significant losses in the adoption experience can they develop a mutual compassion and understanding that will strengthen the familial bond by enhancing their ability to communicate with one another.[3]

Birth parents, it would seem to me, share this role handicap. Forever parents by virtue of their having produced a child, they no longer have that child to parent. The profound loss they suffer is similar to yet very different from that experienced by the infertile couple who experience the loss of their dream child - the one who shares only the best of each of its parents' genetic traits. Both birthparents and infertile adoptive parents must mourn their significant losses in order to effectively resolve their particular life crises. Though the birthparent may have other children and the infertile couple may adopt children, neither is likely to entirely forget the lost child, nor should they expect other children to replace those lost. But once again, we cannot assume the absolute. Just as not all infertile couples find their infertility to be a difficult emotional trial, not all birthparents suffer prolongedly after they make an adoption plan for a child. The intensity of feeling is very individual, and is colored dramatically by the impact of various professionals with whom each will work. Successful resolution of any life crisis will not leave a person embittered and angry, but not all of those touched by adoption successfully resolve this life crisis.

The so-called "Me Decade" of the 1970's encouraged expression of honest feelings and the banding together of those who shared similar problems. This brought a proliferation of adoption-related support groups each with its unique perspective. These groups fought the absolutism of stereotypes of the past. Adults who had been adopted asked society to stop seeing them as "eternal children" and to allow those of them who wanted and needed it access to their own heritage. Birthparents who had been poorly counseled and felt that adoption had been for them the wrong choice called for more thorough and objective counseling, the elimination of the use of fear tactics, the opportunity to exercise more control in selecting families for those children for whom adoptive placement was the best choice, and recognition of their needs as ongoing. Adoptive parents asked for an end to financial, racial, physical, and marital status discrimination in adoption and for a restructuring of policies which consign children in need of permanent families to endless foster care.

The strident militancy of some group spokespeople terrified others touched by adoption as they promoted the new absolutism of their own narrowly held viewpoints, thus broadening the gap between members of the adoption triangle rather than bridging it. As well, the gulf was not only between different sides of the triangle. Increasingly, birthparents who do not agree with other birthparents, adoptive parents who do not agree with other adoptive parents, and adoptees who do not agree with other adoptees have branded each other as "not in touch with true feelings" or "crazy."

Adoption can be a life enhancing experience for all triad members; or it can be a negative and embittering choice. There are no absolutes in adoption, no guaranteed reactions, no universality of needs and feelings. Not all teen parents should make adoption plans; not all infertile couples should adopt; not all adoptive families are happy; not all single parents are less effective at parenting than married couples; material goods do not guarantee an opportunity for a happy life. On the other hand, not all birthparents had babies snatched from them or were inveigled into signing away their parental rights; not all women are maternal and should raise the children they conceive; not all children would be best off raised in their birth families; not all adoptees need to search; not all adoptive parents are terrified of birth-parents; not all birthparents or adoptees need ongoing communication.

It is this absolutism of opinion that this book hopes to erase and replace instead with an understanding of the wide variety of feeling that accompanies adoption as a life experience. Absolutism fosters fear; fear fosters alienation; alienation precludes understanding.

Children are at the center of the adoption experience. As parents - birth or adoptive - all of us wish for the best for our children. We want them to be raised in loving families who will carefully nurture their self images so that they can grow to be secure, happy, loving adults. We want them to acknowledge the realities of life. To raise such children we must as parents acknowledge the realities of adoption - including the fact in most cases, that we do not know the facts. We must ignore the stereotypes and stop inventing dreams about what we might wish for in our children's other parents and prepare ourselves and our children for all possibilities. We must accept their need for information without pressuring them with either more or less than they want.

Noted Swiss child psychologist Jean Piaget has written extensively about his research into the psychological maturation of a child through a series not of ages, but of levels of sophistication. Each child moves through these stages as the maturation of his nervous and muscular systems, the effects of his environment, and his own active seeking out of stimulation and interpretation of events prepares him to do.

Piaget's levels of development have been used by Anne Bernstein in Flight of the Stork, a handbook for parents about sharing sex education with children in tune with their six levels of understanding of the information they will be given. The book is based on her own research with children between the ages of three and twelve who shared with her what they actually knew about where babies come from. Bernstein points out that information shared with a child before s/he reaches an appropriate level of understanding will not be assimilated.

Since "the telling" about adoption is so closely correlated with a child's understanding of where babies come from, children who have been adopted will need, too, to have the facts of their birth and subsequent adoptive placement shared with them at appropriate stages. In this regard, adoption is, indeed, the process mentioned in the definition by Silber and Speedlin quoted at the beginning of this chapter and not just a one time event. You will recall the old joke about the child who came home to ask "Where did I come from?" and was treated to a dissertation on reproductive biology by her mother, who had been waiting nervously for this to come up. Before the mother could finish, the child interrupted impatiently to say "I know all that! But Jimmy comes from Chicago. Where do I come from?"

Adoption is a process, too, for birthparents and for adoptive parents and for the intermediaries who bring these two sets of parents together as well as for the world at large as it touches each of us. From no matter what perspective we come to adoption, perhaps we can agree that we are dealing with a system in need of sweeping change. The change will involve not just institutions, but societal attitudes as well. Adoption should not be eliminated as an option, nor should it be allowed to die. If it is not serving the needs of those whose lives it touches, then we are the people to suggest and work for change. Those who would work for change within this old and beleaguered system would do well to try to eliminate the intra-triad myths and misconceptions which alienate us from one another and to promote an understanding that will allow us to grow together.

I feel pride and deep satisfaction in the direction that this book has grown from its original intent to collect beautiful, positive thoughts. In its final form it contains those beautiful thoughts, but as well it contains thoughts not so beautiful, but beautifully expressed, by those who have not felt adoption to be the same life enhancing experience that it has been for two generations of our family. I feel that Perspectives on a Grafted Tree supports the honest acknowledgement of gains and losses, happiness and pain, that adoption as an experience has on the lives of all whom it touches - birthparents, adoptees, adoptive parents, intermediaries, and the world as a whole.

---

[1] Kathleen Silber and Phylis Speedlin, Dear Birthmother (San Antonio: Adoption Awareness Press, 1982) p. 128.

[2] John Triseliotis, In Search of Origins (Boston: Beacon Press, 1975).

[3] H. David Kirk, Shared Fate: A Theory of Adoption and Mental Health (New York: The Free Press, 1964) and Adoptive Kinship (Toronto: Butterworth, 1981).

BEGINNINGS AND ENDINGS

LITTLE SPIRIT TO CHILDLESS COUPLE

Just helping you, Mom and Dad, to develop
A trait you'll need to survive:
Patience - I guarantee you'll need it
Once I arrive

Carol Lynn Pearson
from The Search

MOTHER'S DAY

I am afraid
To plant this seed.

The sun is warm,
The earth is rich and ready,
But the days go by,
And still no planting.
Why?

The springtime of my life
Is passing, too.
And ten years' planting
In a willing soil
Have borne no living fruit.
So many times I've waited,
Hoped,
Believed,
That God and nature
Would perform
A miracle
Incredible but common.

Nothing grew.
And often times I feel
The mystery of life and growth
Is known to all but me,
Or that reality
Is not as it appears to be.

I have a choice:
To put aside this seed,
Leaving the planting
To the proven growers,
Pretending not to care
For gardening,
And knowing
If I do not try
I cannot fail.

Or plant,
And risk again
The well known pain
Of watching
For the first brave green
And seeing only
Barren ground.

He also spoke
About a seed,
The mustard's tiny grain,
Almost too small to see,
But, oh - the possibilities!
Those who doubt,
Who fear,
Are not inclined to cultivate it.
But it was to them He spoke.

And God remembered Sarah . . .
Rachel . . .
Hannah . . .
Elizabeth . . .

The seed is in my hand,
The trowel in the other;
I am going to the garden
And the Gardener,
Once more.

Margaret Munk
Silver Spring, Maryland
first appeared in Exponent II

TRYING TO CONCEIVE #2

Whaddaya mean, <u>Mother</u> Nature? Nature's no
    mother.
If nature were a mother, women would ovulate once
    a day not once a month And umbilical cords
    would be rigid pipes not flexible ropes
    that can twist and turn and do God-knows-
    what to the baby And placentas wouldn't have
    all those veins and be so complicated And
    it would be impossible for embryoes to implant
    anywhere but the uterus and all babies that
    were meant to be miscarriages wouldn't implant
    in the first place And women wouldn't have
    morning sickness when their babies were
    doing just fine and feel top o' the morning
    when their babies were suffocating
And if Nature were a mother, it wouldn't be
    survival of the fittest; it would be survival
    of the sweetest.
So whaddaya mean, Mother Nature? Nature's no
    mother. If Nature were a mother, there would
    be no "accidents of Nature" If Nature
    were a mother, Nature would be perfect.

Marion Cohen
Philadelphia, Pennsylvania
appeared in the UNITE booklet and in
<u>After a Loss in Pregnancy</u> (Simon
and Shuster, 1982) and to appear
in <u>Moonfire</u>

THE INTAKE INTERVIEW

A closet size interviewing room, windowless
and gray. A middle-aged couple steps in and
sits down. They both look at me, silent,
expectant, hopeful.
They want a baby.
The room is warm. Little beads of sweat are
forming on the man's forehead. He would like
to comfort his wife. After a minute he puts his hand
over hers in her lap.

The fluorescent lamps buzz softly to themselves
and pulse down a blue light that turns
the woman's lipstick purple
and makes us all feel old.

The woman is slight and looks even smaller
as she shrinks in toward her husband.
She begins to shread a Kleenex with her fingers.
The ghost of her unconceived child
stares out at me from behind her eyes.

They have waited to see me for over two years.
I feel weary for these people. I know
their story already. Still, we move through
the desperate routine like
three haggard dancers.

They have been doing biological gymnastics
for seven years. The woman
has taken her temperature every morning
for three years
The man has masturbated
in the doctor's stainless steel bathroom
and then waited
while a technician examined his semen
under a microscope. The numbers seemed adequate
but the sperm weren't very wiggly.

One morning the couple
stayed home from work and made love
at exactly nine o'clock and then
rushed to the doctor so he could
do something to the woman's cervix while
she lay on her back on his
examination table . . . Several times
the doctor even squirted some of the husband's
sperm into her cervix with a plastic syringe,
mixed with the more athletic sperm
of a young medical student
so if the woman ever did have a baby
the man could think that it might be his.

Recently, they have stopped making love
altogether.

They unravel the most private threads
of their lives to me, quivering
with the importance of this hour.
It is almost noon. I am hungry.
I am thinking that I know enough
of these people. I am ashamed

at not having more feeling for them.
An infantryman, after shooting a hole
through his fiftieth or two hundredth enemy
must have similar thoughts. No wonder
soldiers are all crazy when they come home.

The room seems warmer.
The man unbuttons his jacket.
They now offer their professional jobs,
their cultured hobbies,
their gardened suburban home.
"Just look," they are saying,
"See how worthy we are, how deserving."
"See how long we have waited."
"Look," I say back (in so many words)
"I would give you a dozen babies
if I could."

But I have little to offer.
There are no babies now,
I tell them. The babies are all on the Pill,
or sucked out of their cozy wombs
in the tenth week of fetal life.
A few are alive and well and living
with their thirteen year old mothers.

The man and woman eye me suspiciously,
certain that I have a desk drawer full
of babies in my office who I
hand out like lollipops to other people,
the couples who I saw yesterday
and will see tomorrow.

I tell them that I will see
them again in another year. We will have
some more interviews.
They will fill out some more forms.
Maybe there will be a baby for them then.

The man's hair recedes a little further.
The woman feels another line sink
into her forehead. For a moment
they are silent, staring past me at
patterns on the wall.

When they leave
the door clangs behind them
like an echo in a cavern.

Marilee Richards
Oakland, California

waiting for The Call

a saga for Deborah Bonnardel, our social worker,
from an expectant adoptive mother

everytime the phone rings now
my blood pressure soars
my heart drops to my left foot
and my scalp starts to tingle
and with all the serenity of a hungry cat
I say hello in a voice three octaves too high

I unconsciously hum cradle songs
and review old nursery rhymes
because in my bones
I feel the time nearing
as I study spring's calendar
musing on days and dates.

I sit by a green sunny window
in my great-grandfather's rocking chair
and am pleased as I look around
the new calico walls that everything is ready
and it reassures me and makes it real

the calico dog and calico cat
chase one another on a bright field
of yellow and green and orange and blue
and I try to imagine our child, our children

distant laughter circles the hall
and tiny feet run to me
in my imagination as I
sit and rock and write
and wonder and dream and plan

the old rocker squeaks a
comforting old song
and I think of all the children
rocked to sleep in its arms over a century
of all the stories it could tell
of all the family ties that it has bound,
and I am calmed by the infinite cycle of time
and the continuity of life

until the phone rings

Shelia Stewart Darst
Houston, Texas

ADOPTIVE FATHER

I had to be approved to be a father,
While other men didn't have to bother.
I had to answer questions about my life,
They asked all about me and my wife.
They wanted to know if we were wild,
Or if we were fit to raise a child.
I had to bare my very soul
And explain my every goal.
They don't understand what I went through,
Because it was something they didn't have to do.
Most men never have to bother,
But I needed approval to be a father.

Bill Thompson
Spotswood, New Jersey

TO DAVID

I'll take you home with me, my love,
    if only in my heart.
I'll watch you grow, and love, and learn,
    even though we are apart.

My babe, my precious jewel, my own,
    please try to understand
I wanted to keep you to myself,
    but God had another plan.

He meant for you and I to part -
    to bring two people joy -
And he picked you above all the rest,
    my darling little boy.

David, dear, I love you so
    and it causes me much pain
To say goodbye, but I know my loss
    will be another's gain.

I'll never forget the times we had
    when I held you as you slept.
And I'll still feel sad and lonely
    though many tears I've wept.

I love you, David, with all my heart.
    I guess I always will
And when we part, there'll be a place
    that only you can fill.

But darling, as I hold you
    I'm trying not to cry
But it's just so hard to hold back tears
    when I'm saying my last goodbye.

Rosemarie Gross
from I Would Have Searched Forever

OPTING FOR "ME"

Giving up my child
wasn't easy.
Still at nights
I wake with an
ache in my breast
for that child who
I refused nourishment.

But it was either
her or me.

I wanted a chance.
At sixteen love
is often infatuation
and desire knows
nothing of producing
life.

Mama sent me off
to my grandparents
from shame
and my love turned
out to be nothing
more than a ball-point
adolescent exploring.

I wanted me
but she came
forcing her
life out of my clothes
so I gave her to someone
who already had herself.

"My dear daughter
I gave you up
so that you might
grow to like yourself.
Please understand
and love me still."

Opal Palmer
San Francisco, California

CONFESSION

How can I tell you
    Why?
How can I
    Face you - Flower with
    Your father's face, your mother's eyes
    Beloved unknown . . .

How can I state my case, to kill the lie, yet win
    Your pardon - my one judge.
        My son . . .

To begin: I love you. Always, since the first
faint flutter of your life within
    Me . . . But love was not enough, and love
        Was not (no matter what they say)
           The reason Why
             I lost you
              Why
                I left you
                  Why
                      I gave your life away
                Into strangers' hands, into
                  Some official void - I
                  let you fall . . .

Because
    I was afraid
    Because I swallowed lies - their bitter taste
    Remains, taints the years, poisons silence . . .

Because
    I was only Following Orders, only
      Being what was wanted,
    A nice, sweet, Catholic, obedient, passive
      Female Fool -

I was afraid
    To trust my heart, my guts, love-bond
    To say No.
      To defy, refuse to comply
  with what my beaten soul knew to be
      Unnatural Crime -
  Denial of Feeling, of Blood, of Truth,
    Severance
      Of sacred tie.

        Mary Anne Cohen
        Whippany, New Jersey

THE GRAFTING

MY CHILD WAS BORN TODAY

My child was born today.
While another woman felt the wonder of her birth
My heart longed to see her face.

Far away across the sea
She nurses at her mother's breast,
A woman who loves her as I do.
Yet the harshness of this woman's fate
Brings motherhood to me.

Her family broken, mine begins.
Oh, who can understand the ways of life
When loss and love join hands?

Angela McGuire
East Lansing, Michigan

PRE-ADOPTION PICTURE

Infertility insured an equal maternity,
and I first got your photo in the mail
today,
          my instamatic future son.

Eight short weeks of eternity
from today,
          we'll press an airport rail
to guide your landing on the run -

way to our lives. The Boeing bird's hatch
will open and push and deliver
into the cold, foreign air
all that we have in the world:

lost toddler's eyes under a thatch
of black, abondoned hair,
olive hands holding a plastic bag aquiver
with all that you have in the world.

                    Isaac Mozeson
                    New York City, New York

OH, LITTLE ONE

Oh, little one
I have waited so long for you
Come, take my hand
Come, share my love
We have all our todays
We have the promise of tomorrow
Come, let us build a life together.

Ellen Hyers
Catonsville, Maryland

PRELUDE

It is happening again, my child-to-be
An inexplicable yearning,
The compelling longing
To bring you home to me.

Willing you to feel it
I send my love
To kiss your brow
And sing its song within your being.

A wonderous bond has happened, child,
A meeting of both our needs
You need love and a future
And I need you close to me.

Come home soon, my child,
Love's promises await you here.
We've got a song to complete
And a joyful symphony to share.

Elayne D. Mackie
Newburyport, Massachusetts

ON THE NIGHT OF ANDREW'S BIRTH

Strange vigil, this -

My joy subdued
In reverance to her pain
As he,
Traversing unremembered roads of light,
Slips softly
From infinity
Into mortality,
Through her body
To my arms.

Tonight is not for sleep;
It is a night
For fervent thoughts
Projected up and outward
For her,
For him,
For me -

As unto her
Our son is born.

Margaret Munk
Silver Spring, Maryland

I JUST GAVE BIRTH TO A SON

I yell to the desk clerk
in Vermont, the birth
delivered by phone at 7 a.m.

a son, I call
through the door
to my husband
who is asleep

and we hold each other
like children
for the last time
childless

dress in shorts and boots
grin over waffles
fill ourselves with juice

and hike through the valley
where the men plant
their dark patches
with seed

we climb through spring
up the granite mountain
just breaking water
giving life to what it bears
each year.

Judith Steinbergh
Brookline, Massachusetts

PICTURE 254

Flippantly, I turn
wrinkled page over page.
A human mail order catalogue;
broken promises, vacant dreams.
Suddenly, I STOP.
      PICTURE 254
Model - Boy; Color - Olive Brown;
Size - Pint; Used - Slightly;
Smile - Will Melt Jack Frost.
Mesmerized   I feel
your silent heart entwine mine,
strengthening my fleeting pulse.

Like a possessed maniac
I drive myself to meet you;
Ignoring the stop signs
others planted in my path.
The touch of your trepid hand
cools my moist palm.
I sense the pleasant grafting
skin to skin

                marrow to marrow
          soul to soul.
Softly you exhale your past
and inhale our future!

Free of an eighty month gestation
in the frigid Empire State womb,
we ecstatically celebrate
the first seven in one.
A new dirt bike tumbles
a hundred separate times;
silver wheels spinning
elbows 'n knees scraping
a forever son assuring me
  "I'm alright, Dad!"
An old mirror chuckles
at my beard's first gray speckle.

First Grade threatens;
your solemn kaleidoscope eyes
wander into mine, wondering;
"Will our dream be - when I return?"
Limping, you run home wounded
beat up and laughed at -
near the swings on the playground.
  Remember?
You bragged to your classmates
  "I've got a Daddy!"
All day, I bragged, too
  "I've got a Son!"

I kiss your swollen eye,
wash your tear-streaked face
Hold you in my trepid hands;
Cuddled on my lap, I explain
"Son, many boys who have fathers
        NEVER have a Daddy!"
You nod   pretending
to understand our simple mystery.
But it doesn't matter
You feel safe now
Quietly you drift to sleep
in my weary arms.

Eight short years pass -
You're now fifteen.
I recall every picture
my catalogue mind stores.
I taste each birthday
        hear each tumble
        wash all wounds
        sense every graft complete
I can even recount
        every moment of sleep.
I never remember, ever,
you being apart from me!

Richard Stanin
Rochester, New York

ADOPTING FOR ONE'S OWN

The present is a foreign country
to some. We do things differently
here, and he, watching
the landscape out his window - -
railroad trestles, McDonald's - -
landmarks by which he'll remember
his childhood, each passing
silently, darker than dark, a door

closing behind, a curtain drawn.
Say Goodbye, we say, *wave . . .*
Christopher smiles at his new
brother. At five the notion
is quite ideal - - they hug, and if
he had his way, they'd exchange
blood. A long bridge takes us
out of Sandusky across the cause-

way and we lose ourselves in the
north country east of Toledo. Even
with a map we couldn't make sense
of this situation, of the two heads
behind us bobbing like two planets
yet holding hands with a decisiveness
at once embarassing and accurate.
You drive home. I follow

directions. The Honda hunched over
us like an egg, I think we're on
the verge of waking from its blue
dreamy shell. On a fence post
outside Fremont, a ring-necked
pheasant squawks in its own blue
light. Once indigenous to this
area, he's been excommunicated,

and, like an exile, given
to spooky returns. *What's that bird
called,* I ask, and Roosevelt gives
it his name. Ahead, Bowling Green
floats - - an emerald amulet - - as if
retrieved from or surfacing
like England's Lady of the Lake.
Time begins Now, the past

erased. Even on paper
we are his parents, his family.
The chain around his neck shines
like a gold ring. And he returns,
black as a lie, to a life
he's been denied.

Barbara Fialkowski
Bowling Green, Ohio

THE BEGINNING
for Kathie

Into the backbone of a sleet
storm, we headed north to Jacksonville
on the coldest day of forty-six,
that coldest year, to get a baby
sister for me.
              We passed a spread
of azaleas heavy with ice.
The nurserymen knew how to save them:
they had run the sprinklers on them
all night to keep the leaves
from going below freezing.

The ragged bite of February
hung on all day, the slate dawn
sky lingering into morning.
The heater in the old Plymouth
coughed and whined and kept us
cold, Daddy driving in leather,
Mummy and I huddled under blankets.

At the adoption center everything
had been taken care of. We only had
to sign the papers, holding fast
to the words with a ribbon of ink.

I had wanted to help pick her out,
but they know better than we ever
could what was right for us all,
and when they carried her out
just wakened to blankets
unfolding light, we saw her eyes
were ours and knew we couldn't
let her go.

           That coldest night,
we made our way back, moving south
into the flat darkness of palmetto
scrub, three of us bundled
in the back seat, our warmth shared,
and saved.
           We stopped in Deland
for supper. In the diner steam glazed
the windows. The black short-order
cook tested her bottle of milk
on his wrist, staining his brown skin.

How could he have known what held us?

           Malcolm Glass
           Clarksville, Tennessee

FIRST MEETING

He would have said
Go away. But words
were in his future.
Tears came first.

If you had listened
learned from the sounds
of water over rocks
at the end of summer
or in spring after snows
melted upstream
you would have understood.

Like a stranger at Ellis
Island meeting someone known
only by document
I tried to read
this child made alien.
I might have translated
screams and kicks
but he was too wise
knowing I could not fathom
silence   sobbing.
Not speaking his language
my arms were harbingers
to him of home.

People waiting in the station
stared as people do when
someone beats a dog.
The train pulled in after
a fifteen-minute-hour.
What its chug -
chug and whistle
sang to my son
he kept secret
for his diary. Like grass
stirred by a breeze
a smile rippled
into laughter, then rock-
ing to the rhythm of wheels
his eyes riveted the clatter
of a ring-toy sliding back
and forth on a chain

Miriam Proctor
New York City, New York

EARLY MORNING RITUAL WITH A
NEWLY ADOPTED DAUGHTER

In the muted light
your eyes slant upwards at me.
You slouch against the door jamb
fivefoottwoandahalf
in your Snoopy nightgown - -
hair a'tangle,
large mouth slack
your wet goodnight kiss
almost forgotten in the soggy a.m.

I stand at the make-up mirror
pale, blue-eyed,
with lips as thin as a fisherman's line.
I arch an eyebrow with a brown pencil
and step back to gaze at you.
The mirror flings us past recognition

until you mumble "good morning"
in a voice like mine
and we begin again
inventing the temporary cord.

Nancy Cash
Temple City, California

DAUGHTER

I studied you with my hands
that day, just adopted,
coming home from the agency.

searching deep into your hair
touching, probing, like a silly monkey-mother
looking for what? I don't know.

but I numbered your lashes
my thumb smooth across your cheek.

I cupped my hand over your fat brown knee
and rolled your hard toes in my fingers.

I tasted your cheeks and your neck
- you were good -

We've grown older and now you taste like me.
My fingers and your curls are good old friends.
and I even know when it's you leaning
on me, quiet, you and not your sister.

Come. Sit here on my lap.
Your tiny new breasts make me sad.
Come, let me taste you once more.

Pam Conrad
Rockville Centre, New York

WELCOME HOME

Tonight, as you lie sleeping
    for the first time in your bed,
I feel there's something lasting
    and profound that should be said.
But nothing I can think of
    seems quite fitting, so instead,
Welcome home, my child,
    at long last,
    Welcome home.

Welcome home from every yesterday
    from every "then and there"
To the now and evermore
    that's here for you.
Welcome home to true belonging . . .
    to together . . . times we'll share,
And countless family things
    that we will do.

Welcome home to every hope and dream
    just waiting to be yours . . .
To hands that long to guide you
    as you grow.
Welcome home to understanding
    and devotion that endures . . .
To hearts that love you now
    more than you know.

Welcome home to all the memories
    we'll make of every day . . .
To loving ties,
    however far you roam . . .
To joys we'll give each other,
    to the blue skies and the grey . . .
To all these things and more now,
    welcome home.

Tomorrow, when you wake up,
    a brand new life will start . . .
A life in which you'll always be
    a very special part.
So dream sweet dreams . . . and once more
    from the bottom of my heart,
Welcome home, my child.
    Forever . . .
    Welcome Home.

Michael F. Anderson
from Hallmark's <u>Childhood Memories</u>

REACTIONS

WHY THIS CHILD?

Words are like flowers in a summer field,
when I reach to pick them they often yield
unwillingly, or wither in my hand,
limp and useless, not nearly as grand
as before I gathered them on demand.

And today someone asked me, "Why this child?"
"Why her, so foreign and Eastern-styled?
Why do you want her?" The words would not come,
in all that bright meadow of words there were none
to declare the reasons my heart calls her home.

My mind like a new-planted field gently lies,
quietly holding the hows and the whys.
We stand at the deep edge of need, she and I,
across the cold seasons we silently fly
to warm one another, and words don't tell why.

For words are like flowers, delicate, rare
and when I would pick them, are not always there.
As sunlight and shadows on field flowers dart,
or in dim forests ferns flourish apart,
words sometimes don't tell us what blooms in the
        heart.

Lori Hess
from Spokane, Washington,
WACAP newsletter, January, 1976

KINSHIP

Why?
The white-haired matriarch demanded.
Why graft this brown-skinned child
Into your family tree,
A tropic pineapple
Upon a bough of temperate pears?
Choose one at least
Who looks like you.
This one is not your son.

In pride of family,
She has forgotten
To be prouder still;
Forgotten that her family,
And mine,
Is large
And ancient,
And of royal lineage.

She is right
That he is not my son.
He is my brother.

Margaret Munk
Silver Spring, Maryland

Some may be born the whole wide world apart
And speak in different tongues
And have no thought each of the other's being
And no heed
And these, through unknown seas to unknown lands
    shall cross
Escaping wreck, defying death
And all unconsciously shape every act
And bend each wandering step to this one end:
That one day out of darkness they shall meet
And read life's meaning in each other's eyes.

Author Unknown

HOW COULD THEY?

How could they?
Why should they?
Was not their life fulfilled?

Was not the love
Given their own enough?
Was not their obligation -
Conceived with their joining -
To only those brought forth
From the sowing of their own seed?

If they could not bear
We could understand their need
To have a child appearing to be theirs
To nourish, love and raise as their own.

But this . . . ?
How could they?
Why should they?

Their very name is now
Vested in a child not their own
Their souls, twice fused
Into the essence of childhood,
Are now laid naked to a child of sin.

There is no refuge or escape
From the difference of this child.
Their name will not protect them.
Awareness will be the albatross.
Questions the links of chain.

Tolerance will be the repentance,
Shunning the lingering needle of scorn,
Tacit persecution an unchanging precipice
Threatening their lives.

The shunner will strengthen their souls;
The bellicose tire their spirits.
The tightrope, unending before them,
Makes failure a patient foe.

Simple reasons, simple purposes
Will be twisted, mazelike.
Walls will be of scrutiny,
Pathways pitted with doubt,
Openings fickle unknowns.

The anger towards this child's difference,
Like a cancer, will slowly devour them.

How could they?!

W. Steven Hollingsworth
Fort Wayne, Indiana

NOT REALLY YOURS

Not really yours, some people say,
And you'll find out some bitter day.
She'll turn from you and then you'll know
The words I speak now to be true.
Spare yourself the tears, my friend,
    of giving of your heart.
Spare yourself the grief and pain
    of being ripped apart.

Not really mine? You utter fool!
Yes, we'll know bitter days and cruel
And turning away from and turning back,
Of tears and pain there'll be no lack.

But what is love except such things?
There is no joy like giving brings.
To take your child and share your soul
Rips not apart, but makes a whole.

Vicki Andres
Fairport, New York

OUR GIFT

We saw a child miles from home,
Yet distance was not there.
We knew that child was all alone
And that was hard to bear.

And so we dreamt of lovely face,
Of fragile fingers grasping air.
Then we prayed for God's good grace,
We asked Him for His loving care.

He watched our child around the clock,
Until the time was right.
Our hearts could then transcend the block,
We're together through His might.

As parents of this cherished gift,
May we be guided from above.
Never shall our guidance drift,
A family unit - strong in love.

Norel C. Waldhaus
Shelton, Connecticut

STEVIE DIDN'T HEAR

"Black bastard!"
Atrocity
assaulted me
through sultry
backyard suburbia -
ricocheted
across silence
against
thudding blood and
hammering heart.

Not seeing me,
they stood -
eyes firing
soundless
obscenities
at my son playing -
echoing the unspeakable
racial wisdom
of female
WASPolitan
America.
black bastard.

Innocent -
wheels whirring,
training wheels clacking -
Stevie didn't hear.

Grace Sandness
Maple Grove, Minnesota

KITCHEN

How cum you got a white mother?
you told me they asked.
Soapy dish water glistens on my hands.
You are behind me, your face hidden.
And what did you say?
I got mad. I don't like when they ask.
You lean on me, so quiet.
Our silence is like the warm
water soaking these stubborn pots.
Our silence does a job.
Is Atlanta far away?
you want to know.
A few hours.
(An eternity, I think.)
But you are gone when I turn
and I dry my hands alone.

Pam Conrad
Rockville Centre, New York

ADOPTION
(for Sarah)

It happened over night
with a phone call
you became a mother
and one year later mother again:
like driving into a wall,
your whole life as you'd known it
stopped.

You filled out forms,
were interviewed, counseled
and went through more than most of us;
but you missed that slow
growing wonder,
folding into yourself
quiet as never before.

Now you grow sparse, leggy.
They flourish
and with small hands
twist your life to fragments;
you are never alone
can't turn your back -
they're too small.
You bend to chores and long for naps
while they drain
time and attention like milk;
they're so hungry.

You had no idea about the crying.
At night, usually your daughter
wails across your dreams
and alone in the dark,
half awake, pale in your nightgown,
you go to her.
You grab her, squeeze,
try to shake out the crying
the dark need
that tangles
your long black hair.

Carol Burnes
Weston, Massachusetts
first appeared in <u>13th Moon</u>
1979, Volume IV, Number 2

THE ADOPTED ONES

Your oldest son
blows seven candles out.
Of these five, strong, blond children
who would guess which two
were not your own by birth?
They all laugh, tease,
climb on laps. Then Billy
and Jimmy get to wrestling,
Mindy pouts, accuses,
Anna touches the frosting ever so gently
while Jenny sneaks a pretzel
to the dog.

These two, Anna and Jenny.
I guess I would have known.
It's the way they seem to be holding hands
even when parted. The illusion
of fingers interlinked.

I think of memories of darker rooms
before your gaily painted walls.
The voice-shadows, harsh, violent,
but wordless. Wordless.

The nightmares they still have
though less often now, you say,
and less intense.

Now Billy picks Anna up
and swings her around. She yells with joy.
And you say *be careful*. The dog,
grown brave, has his paws
right up on the table cloth
and Jenny is feeding him peanuts.

Hey, Jenny, cut that out, Big Jim says.
Jenny and the dog
disappear under the table.
I hear giggles.

Laughter, happy chaos.
So why, dancing at the window,
do I think I see two shadow-children
standing in the rain, looking in?

Janet McCann
College Station, Texas

THE EASY WAY

The easy way to have a child,
The gossips would agree,
Is just to place an order
And avoid the pregnancy.

Why bother with the nine months wait,
The gain, the girth, the pain?
Why try so hard just to conceive?
It's really quite inane

When all those homeless babies
Wait behind the agency doors.
Why overpopulate the earth
When those kids could be yours?

The easy way to have a child
Is just to order one,
And drive right over and pick one out -
Either kind - daughter or son!

Besides, they say, *God's plan must be*
Both wise and circumspect,
That you will raise the children
That the rest of us reject.

The easy way - no muss, no fuss,
No worry before the birth.
The easy way - no recovery time,
You can hurry back to work!

The easy way? Ah, mavens!
Perhaps you didn't know
The wait has stretched to years, not months,
Adoption is so slow.

And twenty-five eager couples wait
For every babe who's placed.
There are rules and regulations,
Investigations to be faced.

And if we pass inspection -
Are approved for a daughter or son -
We face a years long "pregnancy"
And supervision 'fore it's legally done.

And then we face the gossips again.
Their questions and comments hit home.
Do you know his real mother and father?
How sad there's not one of your own!

Or, *How could anyone ever give up*
Their very own flesh and blood?
Poor baby, he'll miss real mother love.
How kind of you people, how good!

And what if we reach for a different child
With skin of a different shade,
Or a ten year old with a handicap,
Or an oriental maid?

Then it's *How could you ever do that -*
Take such a child to your breast?
The child won't know where his place is!
He'd be better off somewhere else.

Adoption avoids the labor,
But there's pain of a different kind.
There's just as much worry beforehand,
No less apprehensive a mind.

But, then, children don't ever come simply.
There are trials in every way
To gain the treasure of love in a family.
There isn't an easy way.

Pat Johnston

ATTACHMENT

Not flesh of my flesh
Nor bone of my bone,
But still miraculously my own.
Never forget for a single minute
You didn't grow
Under my heart - but in it.

Fleur Conkling Heyliger
from The Saturday Evening Post

TO AN ADOPTED

I
Did not plant you,
True.
But when
The season is done -
When the alternate
Prayers for sun
And for rain
Are counted -
When the pain
Of Weeding
And the pride
Of Watching
Are through -

Then
I will hold you
High,
A shining sheaf
Above the thousand
Seeds grown wild.

Not my planting,
But by heaven
My harvest -
My own child.

Carol Lynn Pearson
Walnut Creek, California
from The Search

TIGHTER IN THE WEAVE

The years of solitude were met
With hopelessness, its toughened net,
That strained out all the optimist,
And kept me off adoption lists.
The loneliness was quite expected,
But never understood;
The emptiness was undetected,
Though never was withstood.

But then your heart mingled in mine,
Attaching substance to its line,
And all the meaning lost in me
Has now become a family;
In your importance I am strong
(It's loving I believe),
To father-mother I belong!
I'm tighter in the weave.

Kirk Shuster
Fort Wayne, Indiana

THE MOTHER OF RED JACKET
to her sisters
September, 1762

They found him hiding in a den of rocks.
He was too weak to bare his teeth
When our men took him from his bed of leaves.
His soft brown hair was heavy with dirt.
Each fevered, trembling, freckled cheek
Was scarred from tears.

              His eyes
Frightened me: blue eyes, wolf's eyes,
Eyes wide and hard from being alone.
I grew cold when he stared at me: I knew
White people are greedy, crazy. I knew
They strike their children.

              But I took him,
That lost little one, and washed him in the river,
And dressed him, and fed him from the kettle,
And placed him among my sons, and I smiled at him
When he pleased me, and when he angered me
My tongue had edges.

              That was all I did.
Now he grows and is strong, and he runs
With my own, and his pale legs flash
As birches among pines, and his eyes
Are warm and soft when I look in them,
For now he is whole.

Sisters!
When he asks me why he came to be here
This is what my heart tells me to say:
Spirit touched us long ago in dream-time,
Little owl, and when winds blew you from your nest
You came to me.

Philip St. Clair
Kent, Ohio

ADOPTION
(to Alex, twenty three months)

Two Jehovah's witnesses in navy blue suits
come up the road,
frightening you,
and you run
to put your face
in my crotch
for solace.

You didn't come out of me,
but you keep going in.
Your smiles,
your bubbling laughs,
your falling over, delighted, with a new word,
your sidelong glance and
chin on clavicle
when you know your're being observed - -
they go into me like knives.

Your whole muscular body goes soft as
a cinnamon bun sometimes.
Across the room
I see your softness.
Your face is a down parka.
The softness sinks in, into me.

Your timidity is mine,
is me as a child.
You put on my past like a parka.
You put on my long eyelashes,
the gleaming satin nape of my neck.
You put on my soft baby feet,
my tender earlobes.

I hold myself by the hand
as the barking dog circles,
as the bush planes roar over,
the strange men come closer.
When I must rinse dirt from your eye,
I am the one screaming
upside down under the gushing faucet.
As the lump rises on your lip,
I hug myself.

Nice knives.
Come cut me up.

Ann Chandonnet
Chugiak, Alaska
from The Wife & Other Poems

MY DAUGHTER'S DOWRY

This you inherit:
The gold of Africa's sun
Bathing a boma of straw;
Gospel singing to close the sores.
And your other part
Chosen to keep the Word
In two thousand years of wandering.
This is yours,
You who came to us
The color of fawn,
African girl,
Daughter of Jerusalem.

Arthur Dobrin
Westbury, Long Island, New York
from Saying My Name Out Loud

GOLD BANGLES: For my Indian daughter

It is twelve years since I first put on
these bangles. Circles
of yellow Indian gold,
they bruised the bones of my hand
as I pulled them on.
I sleep in them; my husband
can tell my mood
from the sound of my bangles
in the dark.

No ornaments, they are
like hair or fingernails part
of my body.
One has a raised design
or spell. The other
is plain, and dented
by my children's teeth.

Daughter, on your wedding day
I will put golden bangles
on your wrists. Gold
to keep you from want
in strangers' houses, and
for beauty: lying down naked
as on the night you were born,
you shall wear upon your dark skin
gold from this distant country
of your birth.

Erika Mumford
Cambridge, Massachusetts

REFLECTION ON LOVE

When I held my first-born
I wondered,
Could any child be more wanted or loved,
But with each successive child the love has grown.
And the love I felt for the newborn babe
is little different
from the love I feel
for the child
who shyly took my hand
and agreed to be my daughter.

Dawn Newell
Canberra, Australia

FOR ANTHONY: Christmas, 1964

For Christmas Gran must make a rhyme
To tell you just how long a time
We waited for a little lad,
(A kindergarten under-grad.)

A boy to cuddle and to squeeze,
A boy to pamper and to please,
Whose tiny fingers, from the start,
Would catch and hold each willing heart.

Whose crooked smile and impish air
Were just the kind you always wear.
A boy so much like you, it seems
We must have kissed you in our dreams.

If Mommy keeps this in Your Book,
When you are older, you can look
At it, and read the verse, and know
It's there because we love you so.

Lola Zierer Beihl
Bradenton, Florida

SONNET FOR MICHELLE
(On receiving Final Adoption Papers)

You shine, Michelle, like sun-sparks dazzle water.
Delicate, feminine, fragile and tough as stone.
Demon, angel, mimic, laughing daughter
Moving like all the music we've ever known.
About our love you curled your baby hand -
Child of our longing, never let us go!
When you are grown perhaps you'll understand
How warm we live within your elfin glow.
A seedling wanting soil, you came to us
For nourishment so you could root and live.
You needed us, but you could never guess -
Small as you were - how much <u>you</u> had to give!
Mountains ring, the wind's a singing bell -
For you belong to us at last, Michelle!

Barbara Nector Davis
Rochester, New York

TO JOHN-DAVID

I wanted none, or so I thought,
The children of others were those I sought.
It was easy to live with such a philosophy
Because for me, bearing a child was never to be.

We worked and we played and we traveled each year,
Then the strange feelings seemed suddenly to appear.
We were childless. It hit us with sadness and despair,
For Daddy and I had so much love to share.

We prayed and we researched the adoption route,
Having realized a family is what life is all about.
Since you came, I have never known such inner joy,
As when I first held you, my precious baby boy.

Rosemary Bleeke
Hoagland, Indiana

MOTHERSPEAKINGS

TO THE BIRTH MOTHER

Your womb opened
I received its fruit
Your son rested in my arms
my son took his first step
in the long man-journey
toward you.

I am grateful to you -
for waiting, yet leaving
messages like pebbles
in fairy tales - this way
through the woods. When he came
you opened your door.

Shirley G. Cochrane
Washington D.C.

TO LEAH

I wear the evidence of your visit
permanent snail tracks about
my breasts and belly
the heart's tattoo
not on the sleeve as some
flashing silver in the sunlight
blue as I prepare for night

I can't remember this body before
you stayed that blink in time
I think that body was mine
firm/ripe flesh
early fruit
the breasts as I recall
were hard and small
this belly didn't exist
but was a stomach then
flat/smooth sand
with a swift tide coming in

This is it now
I can't erase
your love-trace
this is it
this body
this body is it

Christina V. Pacosz
Port Townsend, Washington

FOR MY HUSBAND'S MOTHER

Those months I carried Sara
I'd think of your mother,
the woman who carried you
though she could not
keep you.
       This woman
we do not know, this girl
whose life was changed
in ways we'll never know,
who wanted or did not want
who loved or did not love
who chose or did not choose
but, willing or reluctant
carried you.

Easily, like the grass that sprouts the pasture green
after first fall rains: or in great pain,
volcanic, slow,
the creaking
cracking of the earth, she
birthed you.

We do not know her name
or what she thought as her fingers soaped her taut
belly in the bath,
as your kicks reached her
first uncertain, then
definite, firm rabbit thumps.

We do not know if she could
keep food down, if
her legs cramped,
if she grew dizzy in the grocery
had to drop her head between her knees
to keep from blacking out.

We do not know if she held you in her hospital bed,
if her breasts were bound to keep the milk from
letting down
or if they drugged her and she woke
only to the new softness of her belly, like dough.

We do not know
what friends or family criticized her, if they
sent her out of town and brought her back
as though she'd been on holiday.

We know only
there was a woman who gave you
the food of her blood
the bed of her flesh,
who breathed for you.

We do not know
if anyone ever
thanked her.

Ellen Bass
Aptos, California

IF ONLY YOU COULD KNOW

My son sleeps in my arms now
Safe and warm and loved
And as I rock him, I think of you.
                    If only you could know

Poverty is a thief
Who took too much from you
But life, love and hope
Awaited your son
                    If only you could know

I ache for you
Wishing so much that in your pain
You could know this
                    If only you could know

Our son will thrive and grow
There's nourishment for his body
Food for his soul
And "opportunity" to help make him whole
                    If only you could know

You gave him life
And we will keep that promise
Oh, how I wish you could know this
                    If only you could know

My son sleeps in my arms now
Safe and warm and loved
And in loving him, I love two
My cherished, beautiful child - and you
                    If only you could know

Elayne D. Mackie
Newburyport, Massachusetts

A BIRTHDAY

It's my child's birthday today
He just went dashing by me
His eyes are sparkling with the excitement
      only meant for today
Presents, kisses, hugs, cake, ice cream -
It all seems so natural
It's a day for looking back and looking
      forward.

It's my child's birthday today
But there's something very different
      happening inside of me
This should be a day of complete joy
A day for thanksgiving
But I'm stopped in the midst of all
      this excitement
I'm stopped because my thoughts are with
      "someone" else for a time.

It's my child's birthday today
I have no memories of his life growing
      inside of me and fighting to be released
I have no memories from the beginning months
      of his life
Another "someone" was there
Another "someone" suffered for my joy

It's my child's birthday today
But "someone" somewhere is feeling emptiness inside
I wonder if she is wondering -
    Wondering who he looks like
    Wondering how big - how small
    Wondering if he laughs much
    Wondering if he will wonder someday, too.

It's my child's birthday today
And in the midst of this blessed day
    that was given to me
I have a prayer
    Oh, God that I may never forget that "someone"
    suffered so much to give life to my child.
    That "someone" loved my child so very much in
    that she gave him the right to live. May I
    never forget for a moment and especially now,
    today, to offer a prayer of thanks for that
    "someone", and that you, dear God, can always
    be there by that "someone" to help her through
    the hurts she will have when she stops to think
    that today is "my child's birthday." Amen

Sue Westrum
Glenville, Minnesota

A BIRTHDAY ODE TO WENDY

How do I begin to say
The things within my heart -
The many times I cried for you
Because we had to part.

How do I begin to tell
Of longings down inside
To try to convey the love I feel
That goes so deep and wide.

The many nights I prayed to God
That someday we would meet -
And we'd talk about the missing years
While sharing a birthday treat.

To know your name and hear your voice
Has brought me joy untold -
And as we share and share and share
Our lives we will unfold.

My prayers have been answered,
Thank you, Lord!
You've been so good to me;
I've loved my daughter all along
And only You could see.

The years have come and the years have gone -
But Wendy you never knew -
The 22 birthdays I celebrated
And thought of only you.

But this birthday is different
Because we know it's true -
This is the first one I can say
WENDY, I LOVE YOU!

Sandra Kay Musser
Oaklyn, New Jersey

IS THIS THE DAY?

Is this the day
that a brown-skinned woman
in another land
straightens her back
and stares across the rice paddies
the green carpet blurring . . .?
Is this the day
that brings back the pain?
Remembrance of childbirth
or of separation.
Does she care,
this woman in her faded sari,
what happened to the child she bore,
raised,
but abandoned
when poverty had crushed her spirit?
As I wonder about her,
does she wonder
about the daughter we share?
Oh, dark-eyed woman
in a distant land,
I too feel your pain.
I long to tell you -
She is well,
she is happy,
she loves,
and is loved.

Dawn Newell
Canberra, Australia

THE MOTHER OF MY CHILD*

a baby fills my dream womb
like a full moon opened by tide

it is there
sudden as dawn
spinning toward me

> the mother of my child
> is heaving tonight
> like a spring mountain
> winter is thawing
> from her insides
> she will give up the child
> she will contract
> into a young girl
> wondering at the flood
> wondering at this lost
> territory

A woman calls
official as a head of state
to declare
she is keeping her child
that is all
that is all
the phone withers
in my hand
sleep writhes
out of my skin
like a snake
I am new
to such night cold terror
the breaking of treaties

the mother of my child
is a child
she whimpers
she can't remember
why
she has handed
the moon out of her sky
like a cookie

I reach out
she is smiling
she hands me her motherhood
like a birthright
it is my child
golden as a canyon
for a moment guilt
slides away
like a sweet rain

now the darkness
covers her with ivy
over her flat belly
over her knuckles
over her eyes
feeling its persistant claws
she wills the slow wall
to blot her growing hollow

*for the unnamed women who have given me my
two adopted children

Judith Steinbergh
Brookline, Massachusetts
from Motherwriter
originally published in 13th Moon

DOIN' TIME

Sign the paper here
We need your heart and soul
And your reward is
DOIN' TIME
You will forget
You can have other children
Don't be selfish
You won't regret
You have nothing to offer
DOIN' TIME
Soledad, San Quentin
We all know there are
Other places for
DOIN' TIME
In the night, we feel
The sorrow, the twisting, churning
Of nothingness
The madness of giving, and not
Knowing to whom?
No one ever told us
About
DOIN' TIME

Helen Garcia
Pasadena, California

STIFLED LOVE

I never saw you - Oh, yes, once at a distance.
A small dark head barely peeking from
      beneath a yellow blanket.
It was best this way.
I loved you and still do.
But I can't let that love in my life.
I gave you life so your mother could love you.
I signed papers that said I was "Abandoning" you
But with love,
With knowledge that a family waited for you.
Waited with joyous, outstretched arms.
I've seen the joy of families with special
      babies like you.
It is matchless.
I've no regrets.
You are loved; you are cherished.
Be a good son. Love your mother as my children
      love me.
Show her she's special. Show her love.
Thank her for me for loving you, for giving
      you a place to grow.
I will always love you - But she is your mother.

        Your Birth Mother
        Fort Wayne, Indiana

OUR CHILD

Our child
Can never be not yours,
Nor not ours.

So somehow,
We must let you know
Our unbound gratitude
For this precious gift you nurtured
Then gave into our keeping.

Thank you for sharing life,
For allowing it uterine maturity
In place of abortive non-existence
Which you could have chosen.

Thank you for
Caring deeply,
For trusting enough
To place your babe into a small secure ark,
To float into the rushes of life
Without even a Miriam at watch
To tell you where
His growing path will be.

We honor that trust,
And we shall love and cherish him
As strongly and surely as you do.

Our child
Will grow tall and well,
Undoubtedly with the stumblings
And skinned knees of life.
But always we will be there;
And you also, - in spirit, close by.

A mother's spirit knows no abandonment,
No matter what circumstances
Produce separation or distances.
Our child will always know that you care.

We pray for your joy and well-being.
We humbly acknowledge your gift,
And in spirit closeness
Share with you OUR CHILD.

Chris Probst
West Jordan, Utah

AGENCY POEM

I was promised that they were told
All about me, everything you'd ever need to know
When they adopted you - she had just
read our records, savouring the details, so I
could just fade away, rest in peace, rest assured . . .

That you would grow up with some synthetic story -
absurd picture of well-bred manikins, machines
mating in antiseptic sin, regretting their malfunction,
and delivering the product up for sale
in time to make the last Mass, and go on
to glorious careers - (she was slightly
mad, but outgrew it, and became a missionary
to the crocodiles, he
became a used car salesman, or a used car . . .)
They were both repentant, responsible, white,
very clean, with
intelligence, good looks, and amnesia -
Great potential, if only they could learn
Not to breathe . . .
They did
What Was Right - aren't you satisfied?

And you are supposed to swallow
The whole pill, guilt and all, build your life
on lies (when will they learn
that blood and home are not the same, that neither
replaces the other?) I hope
you will reach deeper, realize
You were never a mistake, pawn, product,
Nameless prize -
You will know
That your mother loved and suffered and was never
repaid for you, that your brothers wait,
father worries, others hope . . .

That you were born to a real woman, real man -
beautiful stupid cruel kind imperfect passionate
human beings, not paper dolls, not machines.

That you are remembered
That your heritage waits in our lives, our minds,
our own words
Not in the dead dust of agency files

That you have as much right as any man on earth
To your blood ties, your own truth
To see yourself reflected
In your mother's eyes.

                        Mary Anne Cohen
                        Whippany, New Jersey

TO MICHAEL, BRIAN, RICKY AND SUSIE

Now you must leave, loves,
To walk where you must,
To fly like an eagle,
To touch whom you trust.

But remember we love you.
Remember we're here.
Remember we want you.
Remember we care.

We know we are different,
Our skins not the same.
Two brown like thick chocolate.
Four white like the rain.

But don't let it scare you,
Cause hatred or war.
It really can't hurt you.
There's very much more.

And remember we love you.
Remember we're here.
Remember we want you.
Remember we care.

We're truly not different.
It's all in the name.
We're all deeply human.
We're really the same.

Our tears flow forth salty.
Our blood, it runs red.
Our hearts can be broken.
Too soon we are dead.

The earth is our mother.
Our roof is the sky.
We all search for God, loves.
We all question why.

So come let us love you.
Let us speak your true names.
And let's be together
Like the wind and the rain.

For freedom will come, loves,
Of that we are sure.
And although we won't chase you,
Our love will endure.

So now you must leave, loves,
To walk where you must,
To fly like an eagle,
To touch whom you trust.

But remember we love you.
Remember we're here.
Remember we want you.
Remember we care.

Kathy Garlitz
Huntertown, Indiana

A FEW DAYS
(my adopted-away daughter turns eighteen)

In a few days
I will be free
From the bonds that bound me
Hand to mouth, to secrecy;

Free to shout and sing
Her name, Louisa, to the wind;
Free to now unbend my soul;
Standing straight and tall,
I'll claim the woman as my own.

I'll not desist;
I will speak free;
Down the tunnel eighteen years
I kept to silence with no speech
To tell the flood tide of my love.

I will speak free;
Just days now,
And she will be eighteen and grown,
No more a child, no more be bound
By oath to facelessness from her.

I will speak;
And call her name;
And tell her sounds to fill the echoes
Where she must have searched for me
Inside herself.

I will tell
The golden story
Of love befell with shame and loss;
Of crowded youth from which I set her free,
Beside myself.

I will tell the lines my face tells;
Hollowed in me, place for her
Now restored to substance.
Her being here will make me free -
Not the other way around.

Elizabeth Omand
Wyncote, Pennsylvania

IDENTITIES

THE BEGINNING

"Where have I come from, where did you pick me up?"
the baby asked its mother.
She answered, half crying, half laughing,
and clasping the baby to her breast, -
"You were hidden in my heart as its desire, my
    darling.
You were in the dolls of my childhood's games;
and when with clay I made the image of my god
    each morning,
I made and unmade you then.
You were enshrined with our household deity,
in his worship I worshipped you.
In all my hopes and my loves, in my life,
in the life of my mother have you lived.
In the lap of the deathless Spirit who rules
    our home
you have been nursed for ages.
When in girlhood my heart was opening its petals,
you hovered like a glow in the sky before sunrise.
Heaven's first darling, twin born with the morning
    light
you have floated down the stream of the world's
    life,
and at last you have stranded on my heart.
As I gaze on your face, mystery overwhelms me;
you who belong to all have become mine.
For fear of losing you I hold you tight to my
    breast.
What magic has snared the world's treasure
in these slender arms of mine?"

Rabindranath Tagore, 1861 - 1941
Calcutta, Bengal, India
from Collected Poems

LEGACY OF AN ADOPTED CHILD

Once there were two women
Who never knew each other
One you do not remember
The other you call mother.

Two different lives
Shaped to make yours one.
One became your guiding star
The other became your sun.

The first gave you life
And the second taught you to live it.
The first gave you a need for love
And the second was there to give it.

One gave you a nationality
The other gave you a name.
One gave you the seed of talent
The other gave you aim.

One gave you emotions
The other calmed your fears.
One saw your first sweet smile
The other dried your tears.

One gave you up.
It was all that she could do.
The other prayed for a child
And God led her straight to you.

And now you ask me through your tears
The age-old question through the years
Heredity or environment - which are you the product of?
Neither, my darling, neither
Just two different kinds of love.

Author unknown

FIRST GRIEF

Last night, my daughter -
Mine by right of love and law,
But not by birth -
Cried for her "other mother."

Accountable
And duly baptized she may be,
But eight is young
For grown- up grief,
The first I cannot mend
With Band- aids,
Easy words
Or promises.

I cannot tell her yet
How I have also cried
Sometimes at night
To one whose memory
My birth erased;
Who let me go
To other parents
Who could train and shape the soul
She had prepared,
Then hid her face from me.

Margaret Munk
Silver Spring, Maryland
first appeared in Exponent II

ACCEPTANCE

So child
there is a woman
you've decided to own,
out of whose womb you came
pink and perfect,
neither you nor I can know her name.
and she was young, child,
too young for a baby like you
and blond and I'll bet pretty
like you are, fair and blue eyed,
not like this dark-haired planet
you revolve around.
At last, you consider the woman
and call her Queen or Movie Star,
too important or busy for babies,
but deep down you know and claim
you're a princess
or the daughter of a Star.
neither you nor I can know her name.

Judith Steinbergh
Brookline, Massachusetts

FOUNDLING

Ah-hah.
I am a magician's trick.
Not born, but conjured,
made not with labor, but a magic word.
Abracadabra was my mother,
my father was a wand.
I swam in the placenta of a black silk hat.
Who in the audience can guess my name?
Close your eyes
Touch your fingers to your temples
and see if we can each take hold
of one end of a name.
Names, I'm afraid, are traits,
like dark eyes, or a love of music.
This is obscured from those
whose families named them.
So the name may not be Susan or Rebecca,
but oak, or savory, or chisel.
Yes, madam, you have guessed. And you,
sir, you too.

Everything you call me is my name;
Say the alphabet, you have it.
I must answer to everything.
You notice, I resemble all of you,
so that strangers seeing me sometimes gasp,
claiming their lost child.
I bear a strong likeness to both bricks
and grains of rice.
I have seen my face mirrored by certain hours,
and begged them to stay, sure we were related.
I have sobbed into the laps of easy chairs,
crying, Hold me, I am your daughter.
I sleep in different beds, and lying there,
naked in the center like a target,
I think: tonight, this night, I may be born in you.
I think: Oh, arrow of birth, come fix me here.

Patricia Storace
New York City, New York

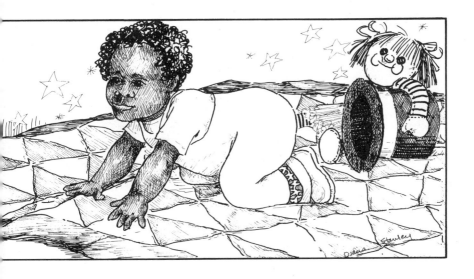

BLOODLINES

My daughter puts her hand
on my wife's belly. I came from
there, she claims. Beams at us both.
Her education sound. No, her mother
says. Remember what we've said?
How we picked you out from all
the others we could have? At two weeks
old you came to us. She's heard,
but never understood. It contradicts
the film she saw today at school.
She shakes her head. Then where?
From the adoption agency. Then how?
From another woman's womb. And what's
a womb? She must have missed that word
at school. Where babies grow. But not in you?
No. Then where? Somebody else. Then who?
We really do not know. Then how
can you be sure? It's the way it's done.
For even me? Yes. Then who's my mom?
Me. I mean the one who . . . You know . . .
Grew me there. We just don't know.
That night we tucked her in
Kissed her goodnight. Peeped in
before we went to bed. Found her
curled up, cocooned inside the sheet.

Walter McDonald
Lubbock, Texas
from Anything, Anything

LOST HISTORY

Heredity is responsible for
my colouring, size and features
and the links to family
are easily recognized -
father's hair, mother's eyes
and grandmother's disposition.
Documents and photographs
for more than a hundred years
give substance to my genealogy.
But you, my child,
have none of that.
It is part of what you lost
before you came to us.
Your own history is unknown.
Not for you the recognition
of shared talents or features,
the feeling of belonging
and knowing your place.
We give you our love
and understanding,
freedom to be yourself
and the support of family.
Our relatives are yours,
yet we know
you cannot find yourself in them.
Your sense of identity will come
in other ways.

Dawn Newell
Canberra, Australia

TO MAMA
(On my birthday)

Where are you, woman?
You who lay spread-eagled
Thirty years ago today
Casting out nine months of me
With a heave and a shove -
Do you remember?
For it was your delivery day.

Did you ever hold that kid of yours?
Take me in your arms?
Or was it an instant's separation
As quick as the snip of cord
That severed us two?

And now do you ever wonder like I do . . .
If my eyes are like yours?
Nearsighted? Lapis blue?
Are you thin like me?
And is the little finger on both your hands
Just a bit crooked like mine?

You have three grandsons;
Their eyes are blue; their hair is fair;
Two are twins almost three
But they call another Grandma
And I another, Mother.

One day I'll come
Traveling my shadow to your door.
"Collecting for the heart fund,"
I will tell you,
Take your dollar
And drive away.

Sue Walker
Mobile, Alabama

The Search: IDENTITY, Out

How can we find out
who we are when we're
composed of so many who
are lost to our discovering

1979

The Search: IDENTITY, In

If I let you
come inside me
too far
you may never get out
what will I
do with you there
crying in the dark
searching for a way home

1982

Marianna F. Gentile
Wilmette, Illinois

MARY CASSATT'S MOTHERS AND CHILDREN

Mother, you were such a cliche,
leaving your newborn bastard child
on the doorstep of a richer, childless house.

Although I was ugly,
covered with blood and disgrace,
you must have loved me -
we were the closest two people can be.

I understand your relief,
to be rid of me.
I brought you nothing but grief,
the scorn of your people
I kept you prisoner for nine months.
I was your shame, realized in flesh.

But do you ever think
how beautiful we could have been together?
We could have been madonna and child.

Look at Mary Cassatt's paintings -
She painted mothers with their children.
She could only paint that vision.
We could have lived it.

Leslie Brooke
Bettendorf, Iowa
first appeared in Literary Cavalcade

MY BROWN DAUGHTER

"Do you know where my mother is?"
she asked,
searching me with sober
dark-lashed eyes,
her 'fro' forked like a halo
'round her face,
"oh-h . . . do you?"

(Somewhere there's a woman
who would know . . .
beautiful, with latin-eyes
like hers . . .
a wordless decade past,
she would remember.)

"Do you know where my mother is?"
Oh, yes.
For eight of her ten years
I've been the one
to share her laughter
to console her tears,
to love her . . .
do I know WHO her mother is?
I know!

Grace Sandness
Maple Grove, Minnesota

SEA POEM

How are we tied?
    Boy on a beach, wave-washed, sky-dazzled,
        Spinning your voiceless dreams, star journeys,
          Sea splendor, whale song . . .

Dreams untold unspoken because
    The only words are waves are water are
        breaking into diamonds into murmur
          into foam . . . wordless things
            You have always known
              speak here
at eastern edge of dry land, soul home -

Let me tell you a story, my dolphin, my fine son -
    Your mother was a mermaid, your father the west wind
        And you
          Are Prince of Shells, Lobster King
            Riding far surf, fearless, sleek seal
            Even in the teeth of storm.

The answers are here, Freedom, the End, the Beginning.
    Taste of salt are all here swirling sinking rising
        To Moon's call, First Mother, Our Lady
        Of the Tides.

I am always with you, swimming just outside
    Reefs of time, of memory, flying
        with seabirds, Running
            in your blood, in dreams, green waves . . .

Peace in my vision of boy on a beach, My mirror - Peace and Hope
        The pain stills.

Look for me some morning, when mist parts dawn sea, Bringing
    Your brothers, Your story, My own face -
            Listen
    The Mermaid sings
                    Only for you.

                            Mary Anne Cohen
                            Whippany, New Jersey

MOTHER MAY I

Mother May I
Touch your hair
and compare it with mine?
Once I thought
that you were floating through life
on a raft of indifference.
Now I know
I know for certain
That you've been disturbed
for twenty one years
by thoughts of me - -
And how I was
And where I was
And what I felt like
And if I knew my alphabet - -
It's all been answered now
And swallowed like a tasteless pill
We are both too deep to cry what we feel.
Mother may you
call me yours, you ask?
Perhaps. You know
this somewhat chops me in half.
Although one part was always yours
I am sometimes a pie
sliced apart
until there is no whole.
Mother may I tell you how I feel?
When I was too young to speak,
You covered your good-byes with a mirage of tenderness
My other life is all that's real - -
And now, you tuck these years
behind the closet of your memory
with a hug and a kiss for daughter.

Now me, I am a different breed from you
I can't forget so soon
All those nights I wondered "Why?"
And cried because my hair did not match anyone's I knew - -
nor my eyes, nor my nose, nor mouth.
I cried then, but now, perhaps,
I have become too deep to cry what I feel.
Like a creature split in two I wriggle now
Without one head and maybe growing two.
For me the world has changed its view - -
Something links us like the day and night
Yet the two cannot exist as one.
Mother may I?
I know I may, and need not ask you.

Marcia Massco
Washington, D.C.

REFLECTIONS

My Naomi,
blood alone
is not alone the truth
I am your daughter
I am Ruth

I will not tell you
blood does not call blood
I will not claim
there is no throbbing in my veins
of Orpah's longing
for her mother's house
her kin
their household gods

But your people
now are mine
I share
your god
Blood is not
the only kind of truth
I am going home with you, Naomi
I am your daughter
I am Ruth

Elizabeth Morgan
London, England

from that point on . . .

"For me, writing something down was the only road out."
ANNE TYLER

all I can remember about that day
when I was told
that I would never see her again
that she was gone for good
or worse
was the fog
the world was blurred
walking around the yard
the sun beating down
and my feet moving
without my telling them to
I was lightheaded but sure
that the sinking feeling inside
the roller coaster in my stomach
would never leave me as she had
I knew I would break down
crack up at any moment
so I vowed that I couldn't
I had to be true to myself
I had to be strong
this would make me strong
I could live through this
I would be somebody
I would show them all

I think I might have told
Iris Germaine that my mother
would never be coming back
but I can't remember what
she answered
and it didn't matter
there was only me
only me in a crowd of people

I was from that point on
irretrievably alone

Didi S. Dubelyew
Long Beach, New York

MY DAUGHTER'S MOTHERS

Your first mother took you,
sick and half starved,
to the hospital
and left you.
You were six years old
and the middle child.
"She not want me,"
you once said
with such deep sadness
that I wept inside.
Two years you stayed
in the children's ward
waiting for the promised visit
and learning to fear the night.
Then with a new status
    Abandoned Child
you were put in a home -
euphemism for a place
where beatings, ridicule
and drudgery
were doled out by the matron
your second mother.
Two more years passed.
You learned to hate
yourself and your mothers.
And I
third and last of them
have no need to wonder
at your anger.

Dawn Newell
Canberra, Australia

WHO LOVES ME?

Who spawned me? I do not know.
    For none will answer for it.
The blame fell where it will;
    And I alone have bore it.

Who loves me? This I do know.
    For there's much I have been shown.
They that took me raised me well;
    And made their name my own.

        Deloris Selinsky
        Burlington, Massachusetts

THE CRADLE IS TOO SMALL FOR ME

The cradle is too small for me.
Bare boughs rustle against the window.

My skin is wet with tears;
Because no one came to see me.
I shiver.

When I was born,
Others turned their backs on me.

Then you said you liked my nose.
You held me in your arms,
And tossed me in the air.

How nice to be hugged,
And scolded, at last,
To be taken into a home,
And belong.

Your eyes soak love into me.

Dainne Drilock
Bloomfield, New Jersey

I am a ghost-written book
My authors' names
are nowhere on my spine
But inside, look - -
the pair
haunt every line

Elizabeth Morgan
London, England

THE CHOSEN ONE

You chose me to be your child
    And took me when others could not care for me
You cherished the life I had been given
    By someone unable to nurture me
You were willing to feed me, clothe me, shelter me
    Most of all you gave me someone to belong to
You sought me out and became my parent
    You wanted me - you needed me - and I needed you
You talked to me, read to me, hugged me
    Kissed me goodnight and let me dream with you.

Why did those others let me go
    Were they too young, too poor, too frightened
Too overburdened or was life taken from them
    Did they want to keep me - or didn't they care
During our years together, I may wonder about
    Those who gave me life - and let me go
But I will think of them with compassion
    Because they made possible the gift of you and a family
What they couldn't give - you did.

You helped me to grow
    You were the tooth.fairy, Santa Claus, the Easter Bunny
You were there with band aids and medicine too
    At birthday parties, picnics and holidays
Trips to the park, the library, the zoo
    You were at school plays, at camporees and graduation
I had you to walk and talk with
    Sometimes you went without to give to me
You always shared - you always cared
    You chose me and gave me identity, pride, and family
You gave me your name - you are my parent.

Virginia Cain
Reno, Nevada

SEARCH FOR YESTERDAY

You have denied me
My birthright
The traditions
History and lore

The family tree
Is surely planted
Someplace and anchored

But I am unearthed
With this unknown lineage
I have no roots

Though my bark
Is aged and tough
My insides still scatter
In a balmy wind's breath

Didi S. Dubelyew
Long Beach, New York

FAMILY TREE

I knew a cedar tree, when I was small
A democratic, back-yard tree, that held
A clothesline up, and minded not at all,
And had a bench beneath where peas were shelled,
And chickens picked, and corn cut off the cob,
And harness mended, if not past repair;
Or, if sometimes there wasn't any job,
A place where people sat to breathe green air.
It was a courteous tree, and dignified,
But one that didn't in the least object
To work, and felt at home with folks who tried
To do their best and keep their self respect.
If anybody were to question me,
I'd say that cedar was our family tree.

Jane Merchant
from Halfway up the Sky

BENEDICTION

Bless this little heart, this white soul that has
    won the kiss of heaven for our earth.
He loves the light of the sun, he loves the sight
    of his mother's face.
He has not yet learned to despise the dust, and to
    hanker after gold.
Clasp him to your heart and bless him.
He has come into this land of a hundred cross-roads.
I know not how he chose you from the crowd, came to
    your door, and grasped your hand to ask his way.
He will follow you, laughing and talking, and not
    a doubt in his heart.
Keep his trust, lead him straight and bless him.
Lay your hand on his head, and pray that though
        the waves underneath grow threatening, yet the
        breath from above may come and fill his sails
        and waft him to the haven of peace.
Forget him not in your hurry, let him come to your
    heart and bless him.

Rabindranath Tagore, 1861 - 1941
Calcutta, Bengal, India
from <u>Collected Works</u>

The heart of a child is a scroll,
    A page that is lovely and white;
And to it as fleeting years roll,
    Come hands with a story to write.
Be ever so careful, O hand;
    Write thou with a sanctified pen;
Thy story shall live in the land
    For years, in the doings of men.
It shall echo in circles of light,
    Or lead to the death of a soul.
Give here but a message right,
    For the heart of a child is a scroll.

Author unknown

READING AND RESOURCES

READING AND RESOURCES

Those of us who are involved with adoption from any perspective owe it to ourselves to make a conscious and concerted attempt to understand not only the perspectives of those others who share with us a "side" of the "adoption triangle," but the viewpoints of the other "adoption triangle" members. This list of resources and readings has been carefully selected to give you an introduction to the broad spectrum of feelings, needs, and issues of all who are involved in adoption - birth parents, adoptees, and adoptive parents. Each of these will refer you to many more sources of information and understanding.

READING

Bernstein, Anne C., Ph.D.; The Flight of the Stork. New York: Delacorte Press, 1978.

Blais, Madeleine; They Say You Can't Have a Baby: The Dilemma of Infertility. New York: W.W. Norton, 1979.

Brown, Dirck, et al; Dialogue for Understanding: A Handbook for Adoptive and Pre-Adoptive Parents. Palo Alto, California: PACER, 1981.

Campbell, Lee H., ed.; Understanding the Birthparent. Milford, Massachusetts: CUB, 1978.

Jewett, Claudia; Adopting the Older Child. Harvard, Massachusetts: Harvard Common Press, 1978.

Kirk, H. David; Adoptive Kinship. Toronto, Canada: Butterworth, 1981.

Kirk, H. David; Shared Fate: A Theory of Adoption and Mental Health. New York: The Free Press, 1964.

Klibanoff, Elton and Susan; Let's Talk about Adoption. Boston: Little Brown and Co., 1973.

Ladner, Joyce; Mixed Families: Adopting across Racial Boundaries. New York: Anchor Books, 1978.

Lifton, Betty Jean; Lost and Found: The Adoption Experience. New York: Dial Press, 1979.

Livingston, Carole; Why Was I Adopted? Secaucus, New Jersey: Lyle Stuart, Inc., 1978.

Martin, Cynthia D.; Beating the Adoption Game. La Jolla, California: Oaktree Publications, Inc., 1980.

Melina, Lois; Adopted Child, a monthly newsletter for adoptive families, P.O. Box 9362, Moscow, Idaho 83843.

Menning, Barbara Eck; Infertility: A Guide for the Childless Couple. Englewood Cliffs, New Jersey: Prentice-Hall, 1977.

Meezan, William, and Sanford Katz and Eva M. Russo; Adoptions without Agencies: A Study of Independent Adoptions. New York: CWLA, 1978.

Musser, Sandra Kay; I Would Have Searched Forever. Plainfield, New Jersey: Haven Books, 1979.

Plumez, Jacqueline Hornor; Succesful Adoption: A Guide to Finding a Child and Raising a Family. New York: Harmony Books, 1982.

Raymond, Louise; Adoption and After. Revised edition by Colette Dywasuk. New York: Harper and Row, 1974.

Silber, Kathleen, and Phylis Speedlin; Dear Birthmother. San Antonio, Texas: Adoption Awareness Press, 1982.

Silman, Roberta; Somebody Else's Child. New York: Frederick Warne & Co., Inc., 1976.

Smith, Jerome and Franklin I. Miroff; You're Our Child: A Social/Psychological Approach to Adoption. Washington, D.C.: University Press of America, 1981.

Sorosky, Arthur D., Annette Baran and Reuben Pannor; The Adoption Triangle. Garden City, New York: Anchor Press/Doubleday, 1979.

Triseliotis, John; In Search of Origins. Boston: Beacon Press, 1975.

RESOURCES

1. Adoptees Liberty Movement Association (ALMA) is a national organization with chapters throughout the country which will offer help to those adoptees seeking a connection with birth families. They may be reached at P.O. Box 154, Washington Bridge Station, New York, NY 10033

2. Child Welfare League of America (CWLA) is a professional organization of child placing agencies which includes many divisions dealing with special needs children, publishing of CWLA adoption-related studies, etc. A quarterly newsletter, Adoption Report is available. Contact CWLA at 67 Irving Place, New York, NY 10003

3. Committee for Single Adoptive Parents can provide information and resource materials and offer support specifically designed for single parents. Reach them at P.O. Box 4074, Washington, D.C. 20015

4. Concerned United Birthparents (CUB) offers support and advocacy services to those who have relinquished a child for adoption and lobbies for reform of adoption laws and policies. Their newsletter, the CUB Communicator can be obtained through them at P.O. Box 573, Milford, MA 01757

5. Families Adopting Children Everywhere (FACE) is a support, referral and education service for adoptive families, with particular emphasis on those families which include foreign born children. Their bimonthly newsletter, FACE Facts, can be obtained through them at P.O. Box 102, Bel Air, MD 21014

6. Latin American Parents Association (LAPA) is a multichapter organization focusing on the needs of children from Latin America by assisting in parent initiated adoptions, sending material assistance to Latin American orphanages, and offering an opportunity for families with Latin American children to support one another. La Palabra, their bimonthly newsletter, is available through P.O. Box 72, Seaford, NY 11783

7. North American Council on Adoptable Children (NACAC) focuses on the importance of families for uprooted children by providing leadership and linkage among adoptive parent organizations in the U.S. and Canada. Among many services: Adoption in America Help Directory, book sales, and a monthly newsletter, Adoptalk. Contact them at 1346 Connecticut Ave. NW, Washington, D.C. 20036

8. Organization for United Response (OURS) is an all volunteer national organization with many chapters offering assistance, support and advocacy for people who have become a family through adoption. A bimonthly magazine, News of OURS is a benefit of membership through 3307 Hwy. 100 North, Suite 203, Minneapolis, MN 55422.

9. Orphan Voyage, a support and assistance service for adult adoptees can be reached at R.D. 1, Box 53A, Cedaredge, CO 81413

10. Post Adoption Center for Research and Education (PACER) serves all members of the adoption triangle through support groups and education. Reach them at 860 Bryant Street, Palo Alto, CA 94301

11. RESOLVE, Inc., P.O. Box 474, Belmont, MA 02178, is a national organization with over 40 chapters offering support, referral, counseling, and advocacy services for those dealing with a fertility impairment. A bimonthly newsletter is a benefit of membership.

INDEX BY AUTHOR